How to play Golf

Chris Plumridge

Hamlyn

London · New York · Sydney · Toronto

Foreword

In my profession as golf writer I am often informed by friends and acquaintances that I must have the best job in the world. Naturally most of these people are golfers themselves with a somewhat rose-tinted view of what my job actually entails, but, after some soul-searching, I have to agree.

I frequently give thanks to that quirk of fate which enabled me to grow up on the edge of a golf course, take my first hesitant swings at the age of six and embark on a love affair with the game which shows no signs of abating in its ardour.

Such is the fascination of golf that men and women can play it practically all their lives and yet still find the challenges it presents as fresh as the day they started. The game requires no great athletic ability nor physical strength and can be taken up at the age of five or 50. Indeed, it is recorded that one Nathaniel Vickers, an American, was still playing at the age of 100. Few games can offer such an extended run to the player.

So what is it about golf that causes such long-term addiction? This book will provide some of the answers to that question, particularly for those people who are thinking of taking up the game or who have just started playing. Established players will need no confirmation of the game's appeal, but even they may find some nuggets of information within these pages that could transform their game.

Sitting here in front of my typewriter, I see through the window that the sun is shining, the larks are soaring high in the sky, the grass is velvet green and the golf course is just waiting around the corner. Why don't you join me?

Chris Plumridge

Contents

cover Tom Watson
endpaper Jack Nicklaus
title page Tom Watson

Acknowledgments
The photographs in this book are by Peter Dazeley with the exception
of the following: Associated Press, London 50 top; Aerofilms,
London 10; Mansell Collection, London 7, 8 top, 57 top; Colorsport, 55, cover.
The drawings are by the Hayward Art Group.
We should also like to thank Beaconsfield Golf Club for their assistance.

Published by
The Hamlyn Publishing Group Limited
London · New York · Sydney · Toronto
Astronaut House, Feltham, Middlesex, England

Copyright © The Hamlyn Publishing Group Limited 1979
Reprinted in 1979

ISBN 0 600 34076 7

Filmset in Great Britain by Tradespools Limited, Frome
Printed in Italy

Chapter One
Introduction to the Game

Origins

It has been suggested that launching a projectile into the air represents man's deep-seated desire to fly and if one looks back through the history books, there seems to be ample evidence of this. While we cannot assume that the English archers at Agincourt were, in fact, frustrated golfers who had not discovered the golf ball, there is a great deal in common between archery and golf. Both require the launching of a projectile at a target many yards away, both are conducted in the open and are thus subject to the vagaries of the weather, both use implements constructed from wood and steel and both require a certain amount of co-ordination if a shot is to be launched successfully.

There are many theories concerning the origins of golf, but finding the definitive one is like trying to discover who invented the wheel. One school of thought may favour the rustic pastime of the Romans, called *paganica*: another may favour the Belgian game *chole* while a third may support *kolfspel* from Holland. All of these games differed in some way from golf, but they all featured that overpowering desire to swing a stick and hit something into the air with it.

I still belong to the archery school of thought particularly as there is documented evidence to the effect that, in the late 15th century, at least three edicts were issued calling for the banning of golf in favour of archery practice. Since these directives emanated from the parliaments of the Scottish kings it is easy to see why the game is generally believed to have started in Scotland and when James VI of Scotland became James I of England, golf's conquest of the world began.

The course

Golf is unique among sports in that the arena designated for actual combat covers such a large area. There are no stadiums or pitches in golf and therefore very few restrictions on where the ball can be hit.

A golf course usually comprises 18 holes which usually measure between 6000 yards and 7000 yards. There are shorter courses and longer courses, but generally they fall between these two distances. Some courses have only nine holes in which case the same holes have to be played twice.

The modern courses one sees today, either at first-hand or on the television,

A young Dutch Kolfer from a painting by Albert Cuyp (c. 1650).

Above 18th-century golfers at St Andrews.

Opposite top Prestwick, site of the first Open Championship in 1860. Note the sleepers from which the ball could rebound into the sand.

Opposite bottom The clubhouse at Augusta National Golf Club.

Below The home of golf, the Royal and Ancient Golf Club of St Andrews and its 18th green.

are a far cry from those in the distant days in Scotland when play took place on a strip of land between the mainland and the sea. This 'link' between the sea and the land was usually common ground and so the golfers of the day took to it, hence the derivation of the term 'golf links'. Gradually the grass took a hold on this land and so play took place between the great

sand-dunes that the sea had piled up over the centuries. These links courses are unique to Great Britain and form an important part of the heritage of the game for they were really constructed by nature with only a few additions made by man. Today these courses, with very few alterations, still set the same problems to the player as they did many years ago and the finest among them, such as St Andrews, Muirfield, Turnberry and Carnoustie in Scotland and Royal Lytham and St Annes and Royal Birkdale in England are the venues for the British Open Championship, the oldest major championship in the world of golf.

With the development of the game, courses have been constructed all over the

Aerial view of Royal Lytham and St Annes
with a championship in progress.

world on a variety of landscapes and the
era of the golf course architect is well and
truly upon us. It is his task to view a piece
of land covering some 100 acres and from
it create 18 holes, each varying in length,
that will provide the player of any standard
with a suitable challenge. It is no easy task
for the architect will need to know the
suitability of certain grasses for the area,
the necessity of good drainage at various
points and many other technical details.
Most importantly, he will need to know
when to leave alone what nature has
created and when to bring in the earth-
moving machinery. He is like an artist
working on a giant canvas and, as with a
great painting, his creative instincts are the
key to a stimulating finished work or a dull
one.

It would take another complete book to explore all the intricacies of golf course architecture and the influence of certain architects on the game. All we are concerned with here are the basics and so we can generalize by saying that most golf courses have four long holes measuring between 476 yards and 550 yards, four short holes measuring between 120 yards and 250 yards and 10 medium length holes measuring between 251 yards and 475 yards. The holes should be laid out to create a rhythm to a round, that is to say the long and the short holes are placed to break up the pattern of the medium-length holes. The holes should run in varying directions so that the wind will come from differing aspects and parallel holes should be avoided.

Finally the architect makes judicious use of hazards such as bunkers, trees, streams, ditches and ponds so that they form the boundaries of a path the player ought to take to the hole. In many instances the architect offers two routes on the same hole, one difficult and one not so difficult, and it is up to the player to select the one which lies within his capabilities.

Rules

Since golf balls have the somewhat un-nerving habit of ending up in all manner of unusual places, over the years a set of rules has been evolved which covers practically all contingencies. The rules of golf, and there are 41 of them framed to make the game as fair as possible, are extremely complex and it is the duty of every player to read and absorb the most important of them. In Great Britain, the governing body of the game has its head-quarters at the Royal and Ancient Golf Club of St Andrews; in the United States it is the United States Golf Association, based in New Jersey. These two bodies deal with all the rules queries which crop up around the world because in spite of those 41 rules, instances still occur that are not covered by a specific rule.

To familiarize yourself with the rules of golf, you should contact the above organizations, the Royal Insurance Company of London who produce a small booklet containing the rules or your nearest golf club secretary who will have a copy of them.

Etiquette

Etiquette on the golf course is simply good manners. Golf is a quiet game played at walking-pace; therefore any action which disturbs that tranquillity is a breach of etiquette. Your first consideration should be for your fellow-players and it is a case of do as you would be done by. Do not move or talk when your opponent is about to make his stroke; do not stand too near or on-line with your opponent, always try and stand several feet to the side; do not shout across the course to a friend playing on another hole, your shout could put off a player on the hole in front of you. Always walk at a reasonably brisk pace; do not loiter as this could hold up the people playing behind you. Should you lose a ball, always wave the players behind you to come through – slow play is the bane of modern golf and anything you can do to speed it up will help. If you take a divot with your shot, always replace it, always repair your ball pitch-marks on the greens and always, without fail, repair your footmarks after you have played from a bunker. There is nothing worse than finding your ball in a bunker lying in the footmarks of some inconsiderate player who was there earlier.

If you are concerned about golf etiquette, simply watch what established players do and learn by example, but by and large etiquette on the golf course is purely a matter of courtesy and common sense.

Scoring systems

Scoring in golf is another part of the etiquette. There are no umpires or referees to give a decision, the player is alone with his conscience. Cheating at golf is simply

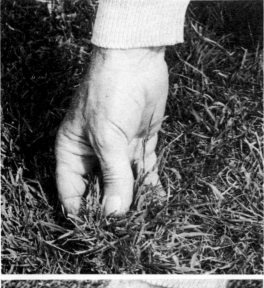

Always replace divots, repair pitch marks on the green and smooth footprints in bunkers.

not tolerated and should a player cheat and be discovered, which he will be eventually, then he will be branded for the rest of his golfing days and will be avoided by his fellow players.

Breaking the rules inadvertently is another matter and happens frequently through misinterpretation. In these cases the player is penalized under the rule applying to the situation.

There is only one form of scoring used in golf and that is to count the number of strokes made at the ball and that includes attempts to hit the ball that miss altogether! There are a number of systems to which scoring can be applied. The most popular is called stroke-play whereby each player counts every stroke he makes and the player who, at the end of the day, has played the least number of strokes is adjudged the winner. In stroke-play every hole must be completed by the player putting his ball into the hole.

The other favoured system is match-play in which the players play individually against each other rather than the rest of the field. In match-play, if player A holes out in five strokes and player B holes out in six strokes then player A wins the hole. The match proceeds in this fashion until one player is more holes ahead than there are holes left to play. Thus, a result which reads that player A beat player B by three and two means that A was three holes ahead with only two left to play and therefore was unbeatable. It often happens in match-play that at the end of 18 holes the players are level or, in golfing terminology, 'all square'. If a result has to be achieved then the players return to the first hole and the first player to win a hole is the winner. This is known as 'sudden-death' and from this a result may read that player A beat player B at the 19th or the 21st or even the 24th, depending on the number of extra holes they played before a player won a hole. In match-play the ball does not have to be holed out as a player may consider that his opponent's ball is so close to the hole that it would be impossible to miss and he can concede the putt.

There are variations on both these forms of play whereby two players can play in partnership as a team against two other players or as a team against a field of teams. Foursome golf is played with the two partners hitting alternate shots and driving on alternate holes: four-ball golf is played with the best score on a hole from one team counting against the best scores from each of the other teams.

Other forms of scoring include a points system of scoring known as a Stableford. This form, invented by Dr Frank Stableford, awards points for the number of strokes taken at each hole. One point is scored for a hole completed in one over par, two points are awarded for a par and three points awarded for one under par (known as a birdie) and so on. Players can also play a Bogey competition in which the player competes against the par of the hole in match-play form. If a player scores a par then he has halved the hole, if he scores over par he loses the hole and if he scores below par he wins the hole. The player who is the most ahead of par or the least behind par at the end of the day is the winner. All the forms of scoring used in golf are fully explained in the rules of golf.

Handicapping
Whatever the type of competition, the object of the game, as you probably know, is to get the ball into the hole in the least number of strokes. What this number actually becomes is dictated by the ability of the player and the distance he has to cover on each hole.

Each hole on an 18-hole course is given a rating depending upon its length. This rating is called 'par' and is the number of strokes a very good player, in his normal form, would take to hole out. All holes up to 250 yards in length are rated par three: holes between 251 yards and 475 yards are rated par four: holes 476 yards and over are rated par five. If you take our standard course of four par three holes, four par five holes and 10 par four holes the total par for the course adds up to 72. Some courses that are shorter in total length are rated lower, others that are longer are rated higher.

The par of the course acts as the yardstick by which a player judges his performance and thereby gains his handicap. A very good player would go round in an average of 72 strokes over a period of time. This means his handicap would be 0 or 'scratch' as it is called. Some exceptionally good players may go round in an average of two or three strokes under par in which case their handicaps would be plus two or plus three. The majority of players do not reach these exalted heights and their

HANDICAP								HANDICAP				
HOLE	MINIMUM YARDS	MAXIMUM YARDS	PAR	HANDICAP RATING			HOLE	MINIMUM YARDS	MAXIMUM YARDS	PAR	HANDICAP RATING	
1	365	400	4	9			10	445	485	4	6	
2	475	555	5	1			11	345	445	4	12	
3	340	360	4	11			12	130	155	3	16	
4	170	220	3	15			13	455	485	5	4	
5	410	450	4	5			14	390	420	4	8	
6	160	190	3	17			15	465	520	5	2	
7	315	365	4	13			16	125	190	3	18	
8	465	530	5	3			17	345	400	4	14	
9	380	440	4	7			18	380	420	4	10	
OUT	3080	3510	36				IN	3080	3520	36		
SCORER							TO'L	6160	7030	72		
ATTEST			DATE							NET SCORES		

Minimum distances as shown represent yardage from front of tees to nearest pin locations. Average playing length from members tees is approximately 6500 yards. Maximum distances represent measurements from back of tees to the farthest pin locations. Average playing length from championship tees is approximately 6850 yards.

A typical scorecard showing hole length, par and stroke index.

A complete set of clubs showing four woods, nine irons and a putter.

handicaps range from scratch to 24, which is the maximum for men. The maximum for women is 36.

Thus, an 18-handicap player is one whose average score is 90 on a par 72 course. You can see that it is possible for an 18-handicap player to compete with a scratch player by use of his handicap.

In stroke-play the full handicap is deducted from the gross score and the winner adjudged on the lowest net score. In match-play a percentage of strokes is given by the lower handicap player to the higher handicap player. For instance, if player A is 6-handicap and player B is 18-handicap then the difference is 12 strokes, but player A is only required to give three-quarters of the difference, so player B would receive nine strokes. This means that on nine holes of the course player B would subtract a stroke from his score before comparing it with A's score. To find out where these strokes are taken, the players look at the scorecard for the column marked stroke index. Every hole with the number nine or less marked against it would indicate, in this example, where the strokes are to be taken.

This equation is used whatever the difference between handicaps. If the difference results in a fraction, for instance 4½, then it is rounded up to the nearest number, in this case five. Handicapping means that golfers of all standards can compete against one another with everyone having an equal chance. The only players who do not have a handicap are professionals, who are all rated as scratch and compete with one another on that basis.

Equipment
A full set of golf clubs contains 14 clubs, which is the maximum under the rules that can be carried during a round. Sets can be purchased from any golf club professional who will also be able to advise you on the type of clubs which will suit you best. Golf clubs are expensive items and if you are just beginning the game it is often advisable to purchase what is termed a 'short set' which comprises just seven clubs. This number will be perfectly adequate for your initial needs. In many cases, the professional will have second-hand sets among his stock and these are also worth considering. Golf clubs are divided into two types— woods and irons, referring to the clubhead. As suggested by these names, some are made of wood and some of iron with the shaft usually made of steel. In a full set of clubs there are usually four woods and 10 irons, one of which is a putter. Each club is numbered although the woods also retain their old names. Thus the number one wood is called a driver, a number two wood a brassie and a number three wood a spoon.

The numbers on all clubs denote the degree of loft on the clubface. The loft determines the distance and trajectory a golf ball can be hit. A driver or number one wood has very little loft, about 15°, and it is the longest club in the set, measuring about 43 inches in length. This club is designed to hit the ball a long way from the teeing ground with a fairly low trajectory. The two, three and four woods are progressively shorter than the number one wood and have correspondingly greater degrees of loft; consequently the ball will fly higher and not travel so far when hit.

The same applies to the irons which are numbered one to 10. A 1-iron has hardly any loft and really is a club for the very advanced player. The same applies to a 2-iron and so most average players start their sets with a 3-iron. The set progresses from 3-iron to 9-iron with each club having a little more loft and the length of the club becoming shorter. After the 9-iron come two other clubs called the wedge or 10-iron and sand-wedge. These clubs have extreme degrees of loft and are used for hitting the ball short distances with accuracy. As the name sand-wedge implies, this club is specially designed for hitting the ball out of bunkers or sand-traps as they are sometimes called. Modern golf club design has made great strides in recent years and provides the golfer with sophisticated weaponry to help his game, but the principles remain the same. Each club is designed for a specific use, that is to hit the ball a required distance. It is difficult to give the exact distances each club hits the ball because that depends on the player swinging it, but once a player has established his maximum distance with the driver all other clubs should follow in progression. A top-class professional can hit a driver an average of 260 yards—he may hit some drives over 300 yards or some of 240 yards, but normally he will be between those figures. He would hit a brassie maybe 10 yards

less, a spoon 20 yards less and a four wood 40 yards less. He would hit a 3-iron about 200 yards and all other iron clubs would progress downwards by 10 to 15 yards so that he would hit a wedge about 100 yards.

The amateur golfer may only average 200 yards with his driver so the distance he hits with each of the other clubs would be correspondingly shorter. All players learn how far they can hit with each club and, using their judgment, select the club they feel will cover the distance required.

Now we come to the final club in the bag—the putter. This is used on the greens for rolling the ball along the ground and into the hole. This club has hardly any loft at all. Putters are made in various shapes and sizes and choosing a putter is largely a matter of what looks and feels right for you.

If you choose a short set to start with you should again consult a golf professional who will assist you. You should choose the number two and four woods and numbers 3, 5, 7 and 9 irons plus putter. As you gradually become more proficient you will be able to add the rest of the clubs.

Although golf clubs represent the largest initial outlay in starting the game, the

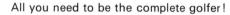

All you need to be the complete golfer!

a little further than the American ball.

You will also need a golf bag to carry your clubs, balls, umbrella, tee-pegs, waterproofs and other sundry items. If you buy a large bag you will also need a trolley to help you pull the bag round the course. You can, however, buy a slimmer bag which you carry on your shoulder and this type of bag has found favour recently as it aids faster play.

Now we come to clothing and footwear. You will need two pairs of shoes, one for heavy winter wear and the other for summer play. Golf shoes are designed to help you maintain a good balance during your swing and have spikes for this purpose. They should support your feet properly and not be too heavy. Since a player covers over five miles during a round, it is vital to have good-fitting shoes. Never play a full round in new shoes—the blisters you develop will keep you off the course for days. Gradually break them in by wearing them for short distances or when you go on the practice ground.

Fashions for golfers have really advanced and the days of turning up to play in your old gardening trousers topped off with a moth-eaten sweater have gone.

Above Waterproof trousers are essential for playing in the rain as Johnny Miller appreciates.

Right Attractive professional golfers like Sally Little have helped boost women's golf.

purchasing does not, unfortunately, stop there. You will need some golf balls, probably three or four dozen, but you can buy practice balls or 'seconds' which are cheaper. There are two sizes of golf ball available, the larger American size and the smaller British size. The difference in size is small, the American ball being 1·68 inches in diameter and the British ball 1·62 inches. British golfers can choose which they like, but when starting the British ball is more satisfying since it flies

Now you can buy colour co-ordinated trousers, sweaters and shirts which are designed for the golfer. Sweaters and shirts should have plenty of room under and around the arms for freedom of movement and should be long enough to cover the lower back area. Back injuries are common in golf so it is advisable to keep that area as warm as possible to avoid muscle injury through cold. If you wish you can complete the ensemble with a cap or a hat and it is wise to at least carry one in case of rain. Since golf is played in the rain, you should also equip yourself with an umbrella and waterproof trousers and jacket.

The final item is what might be termed an optional extra and that is a left-hand glove. This was popularized by the great British player Henry Cotton, who wore one throughout his career. The glove helps the player retain a firm grip throughout his swing.

It is important that you try and look like a golfer for psychological reasons—if you dress sloppily you'll play sloppily, if you dress well you have a better chance of playing well.

In this explanation I have described equipment available for the right-handed player and this book is written for the right-handed player. There is nothing discriminatory about this, it is simply that the majority of players are right-handed. Left-handed players are fully catered for and matched sets are available for them. One small point concerning the glove—a left-handed player will need a glove for his or her right hand.

As I stated in my Foreword, golf is a game to be enjoyed by both men and women and in recent years there has been a tremendous upsurge in the growth of women's golf. All major golf club manufacturers produce sets of clubs designed for women and there is also a comprehensive range of clothing available to help women look attractive and feminine on the course.

If you are starting golf then the initial outlay is quite high, but your clubs will last several years and the pleasure you will derive from the game will far outweigh the cost. Your local golf club professional will have all this equipment in stock and a visit to his shop is absolutely necessary in order to obtain the correct advice on exactly what you should purchase.

Chapter Two
The Swing Foundations

The object of the golf swing is to generate power at the precise moment when the clubhead is striking the ball. This power must also be generated accurately so that the clubhead is travelling along the correct path to propel the ball in the right direction. In order to achieve these two ob-

A natural stance with the feet square to the intended line.

jectives, the golfer has to make certain movements that are designed to help him in his quest for power and accuracy.

These movements, however, will be useless if the foundations upon which they are built are insecure. To begin with, a golfer must master the swing foundations for without that mastery he will never realize his full potential. It is not as difficult as it may appear to master the swing foundations as they all take place before the club is actually set in motion. All the swing foundations complement each other and enable the golfer to combine them into the execution of a free-flowing, powerful swing.

The stance
Good golf starts from the feet and since they are your only contact with Mother Earth it is important to use them correctly. A great deal has been written about the stance in golf and most of it is really unnecessary and confusing.

One school of thought maintains that the golfer should stand with his legs apart so that the distance between his feet is the same as the width of his shoulders. This, I think, is confusing particularly if a player has very broad or very narrow shoulders. How you stand to the golf ball should be how you stand in everyday life; in other words, be natural. When you stand with your feet apart at a dance or waiting for a train, you aren't wondering if your feet are the width of your shoulders apart; you simply stand in the position that feels most comfortable to you. So it is when standing to a golf ball. If you are slightly splay-footed when you walk this will be reflected in your golf stance and if you are slightly pigeon-toed then this also will be mirrored in your stance. Don't worry, just be natural and stand with your

weight evenly distributed between your feet in the position that feels most comfortable. Similarly, it is most unlikely that you stand normally with your legs absolutely ramrod straight, yet so many golfers do just that when they come to play. The legs should be relaxed and the knees should be slightly bent as if you were about to sit down.

The position of your feet is also important. Again, if you stand naturally you will probably find that your big toes are parallel. This is called a square stance because your feet are square to the intended line of flight. The lining up of your feet will determine how the rest of your body lines up to the line of flight so it is important to achieve a square stance.

The grip

Your hands are the only contact with the club and how you position them will determine how you hit the ball. The object of the grip is to weld the hands together so that they function as a unit. If your grip does not allow this to happen then you will always struggle. The word 'grip' is something of a misnomer as it implies vice-like clenching of the club when in fact the pressure your hands apply should be no more than is necessary to swing the club back and down again.

The three types of grip: The overlapping, the two-handed and the interlocking.

There are three types of grip you can use. First there is the overlapping grip or 'Vardon grip', so called because it was popularized by the late Harry Vardon, the great British golfer who won the British Open Championship a record six times. This grip involves the little finger of the right hand overlapping the index finger of of the left hand. Then there is the two-handed or 'baseball' grip in which there is no overlapping and both hands are simply placed on the shaft. Lastly, there is the interlocking grip in which the little finger of the right hand and index finger of the left hand interlock. The most popular of these grips is the overlapping grip, but for people with small hands the interlocking grip could be more suitable. The interlocking grip is used by Jack Nicklaus and you won't find a higher recommendation than that. The two-handed grip is favoured by players who have weak hands, but because there is no connection via the fingers between the hands, this is the grip that is most likely to break down.

As the overlapping grip is the most popular we will concentrate on that. Take a club (remember to wear your left-hand

glove) and, adopting the stance we've previously talked about, rest the clubhead on the ground. Now lay the club diagonally across the palm and fingers of the left hand so that the top of the shaft is snug into the palm. Now close your fingers around the shaft and place your left thumb on the shaft so that it is a little to the right as you look down. You should be able to see two to $2\frac{1}{2}$ knuckles of the first three fingers of the left hand when you look down your extended arm.

The right hand is then placed slightly under the shaft so that the fingers wrap around with the little finger overlapping the index finger of the left hand. The thumb of the right hand should be slightly to the left of the shaft and as a further check look down at your hands on the shaft and notice the two 'Vs' formed by the thumb and index finger of each hand. If the 'Vs' are both pointing in the direction of the right shoulder, then your grip is sound. If the 'Vs' point in different directions then your grip is wrong.

Posture

Having learned how to grip the club correctly, you now have to blend that grip into your stance so you are in a position to hit the ball. You will probably find that the club is not long enough to reach the ground even if you are of only average height and your instinct will be to bend from the waist in order to get the clubhead flat on the ground. This is a very common posture among golfers, but remember the flexed knees and sitting down position we talked about earlier. If you remember to keep your upper body as erect as possible

Left A perfect address position: The two 'Vs' formed by the grip point towards the right shoulder, the right shoulder lies lower than the left and the ball is opposite the inside left heel.

Right Four address positions by top-class players: Gary Player, Jack Nicklaus, Hale Irwin and Laura Baugh. Note the flexed knees and arms hanging freely away from the body.

and bend your knees slightly, you will find that the clubhead reaches the ground easily. Remember also the position of the feet because golfers have the habit of lining up their shoulders with their feet. If your feet are square to the intended line of flight then your shoulders have a good chance of being the same.

Your grip can also affect your shoulder position. If your grip with the right hand is too much on top of the shaft, that is too far to the left, then you will find your right shoulder has come round and your shoulders will point to the left. If you get the 'Vs' of your grip pointing back up towards the right shoulder then your shoulders will be in a good position so that when you turn your head to the left you should be looking directly down the intended line of flight. Because the right hand is lower than the left hand on the shaft, your right shoulder will be lower than your left. This posture will also throw a little more weight to the **right**.

Having got into this position with your grip on the club firm but not tight, just swing the club back to about knee height and through again. Imagine you are swishing a stick at a daisy and while you are swinging the club to and fro, try and keep it on a straight path. This will help you get the feel of swinging with your arms and assist your co-ordination.

Ball position
Now you are in a comfortable address position, you have to add the ball which is the chief object of your intentions! The position of the ball in relation to your set-up is vitally important and often overlooked even by experienced players.

Draw an imaginary line from the inside of your left heel at address; where that line meets the clubface is where the ball should be. If you cannot imagine a line, place a club shaft on the ground and then take up your address position with your left heel against the shaft and the shaft at right angles to your intended line of flight. You cannot use the shaft as a guide in actual play as it is against the rules so it is best to get used to positioning the ball on the inside of the left heel without the club shaft.

This ball position should be adopted for all shots (other than specialist shots which we shall deal with later) from those with the driver to those with the 9-iron. Your comfortable stance will be at its widest with the driver and as you progress to the shorter clubs, your stance will become narrower by the simple means of moving your right foot nearer your left. By the time you are playing a 9-iron, your heels will be only a few inches apart, but the ball will still be in line with the inside of your left heel.

Chapter Three
The Swing

If your swing foundations are solidly built then you are well on the way to a sound golf swing. As the word implies, the swing is a continuous action and should always be thought of as such. The hardest part of the swing is actually starting it off for there is nothing to stimulate your action. A squash or tennis player has a moving ball coming towards him and the speed the ball approaches triggers the player's reactions. In golf, the ball is stationary and has to be hit in cold blood. So how do you start the swing that will propel the ball far down the fairway in the intended direction?

In the previous chapter I talked about swinging a club, say a 7-iron, back and forth to about knee height. That exercise was to help you obtain a feeling of what it is like to hold a moving club. The full golf swing is really a matter of building on that action, gradually increasing the length of backswing until you are creating the maximum arc. This action is performed primarily with the forearms and hands and should be maintained at a slow, steady pace.

As the length of the swing increases back and forth you will notice other parts of your body responding to your action. Your left shoulder will be pulled round under your chin and this pulling action will be felt in your left leg. As you bring the club down, the reverse will happen and your right shoulder will come under

your chin and your right leg will be pulled towards your left side. All of this takes place with the head acting as a central pivot. If your head moves to the right as you take the club back then the whole effect will be ruined. Remember, the head acts as a central pivot around which the arms and shoulders revolve.

The pace of your backswing should be as slow as you can possibly make it. What you are trying to do is build up momentum by coiling your body like a spring and then uncoiling to bring the clubhead into the ball at maximum speed. It is clubhead speed that gives your shots distance. The slow backswing allows the big muscles of your shoulders, back and legs to be used to create that coiling action. The smaller muscles in the arms and hands should be kept passive on the backswing, their role will be fulfilled later.

At the moment you are practising your swing without a ball because you are trying to achieve the feel of the golf swing. Do not try and hit a ball until you feel you have control of the club throughout the swing.

If you take the club back as far as you can while keeping the left arm reasonably straight, your left shoulder will be tucked in under your chin. This action will pull your left knee into your right leg and this has the effect of transferring more weight onto the right side. Your hands will be pushed upwards and you will notice that the momentum of the club going back has caused the wrists to cock. This cocking of the wrists happens without any con-

One of the best swings in the modern game. Johnny Miller demonstrates the essence of a full shoulder turn with the hands high at the top. From here he releases that pent up power into the ball and on to a full finish

Above The ageless swing of Sam Snead still retains its graceful rhythm and ease of striking.

scious effort, but it should only occur near the top of the swing. The cocking of the wrists also points the club towards the target at the top of the swing. The position of your left wrist at the top of the swing will tell you which way the club is pointing. If your wrist is cupped then the club will be pointing to the right of the target and the path the club travels through the ball will be across the intended line of flight in a right to left direction. If your left wrist is bowed at the top of the swing then the club will point to the left of the

target and the path the clubhead travels through the ball will be across the intended line of flight in a left to right direction. In effect, the cupped left wrist position will cause a slice and the bowed left wrist position will cause a hook.

The ideal position is for the back of the left hand and wrist to be in a line as this

Below The problems of a tall man are evident in the swing of Peter Oosterhuis, 6ft 5in, who is the tallest player currently competing on the American circuit. At the top of the swing the club is laid off across the target line. From here Peter gets into a good impact position, but the follow-through shows how the shoulders have dominated the swing. Compare this finish position with that of Jack Nicklaus on page 27.

Left Gary Player at the top of the swing. The left wrist and arm are in line and the club shaft is pointing at the target.

Centre Hubert Green just after impact. His weight has moved to the left side with the right knee kicking in. The head is still behind the ball and the left arm and side have remained firm.

Right Tom Watson's well-balanced follow-through.

means the clubhead is pointing towards the target and will travel through the ball along the intended line of flight. Once you have reached the top of your swing with your weight transferred easily onto your right side, the downswing becomes a reflex action to what has gone before, only with the emphasis on the lower half of the body. On the backswing you coiled the top half of your body, on the downswing you uncoil the lower part. Your initial movement for the downswing should be a fast transference of weight onto the left side. You can only do this if your right leg remains flexed at the top of the swing and does not straighten. The flexed but firm right leg enables you to slide your knees and hips towards the left on the downswing. This sliding action also initiates the

pulling down of the hands and arms and as your weight moves through onto your left side, your hands and arms are pulled down and past the ball by the centrifugal force your leg action has created. This centrifugal force also causes the wrists to uncock in an unconscious manner thereby releasing all the pent-up power your body turn has created so that the clubhead is moving at maximum speed as it strikes the ball.

As your arms swing through the ball they will naturally pull your remaining body weight to your left side and your head will gradually be pulled up so you will be looking in the direction the ball has gone. This is called the follow-through and its role is important as a guide to what has gone before in the swing. If your follow-through is unbalanced and your arms are waving around then something has gone wrong with the swing. A smooth, well-balanced follow-through is indicative of a smooth, well-balanced swing.

If you check back with the swing foundations, you will see the part each of them plays in setting you up correctly for the swing:

1) The stance determines the direction you

face and therefore, the path the clubhead will follow. It also controls your footwork through the swing, allowing your legs to respond to the movements your swing creates.

2) The grip allows you to maintain firm control over the club during the swing.

3) Your posture allows you to make your body movements in the correct sequence and also determines the path along which the club travels.

4) The position of the ball just inside the left heel means that the clubhead strikes the ball at the bottom of your swing arc when the clubhead should be travelling at its maximum speed and on its straightest line.

Now you are ready to swing at a golf ball. Use a 7-iron and remember that you hit the ball away from you. The ball is there to be hit, so don't 'baby' it.

As I mentioned earlier, it is difficult actually to start the swing from a static position. What you have to do is break down the static start with a small, almost imperceptible movement. One of the tricks the top professionals use is what is known as a 'forward press'. This is a movement they make to initiate the backswing. Gary Player has a very noticeable action whereby he kicks the right knee into the left, whereas Jack Nicklaus and Sam Snead have less noticeable actions whereby they slowly turn their heads an inch or two to the right as they move the arms back. Nicklaus, in fact, also firms his hands on the grip as his initial movement and the slight head turn follows directly afterwards. Some players favour a slight push forward with the hands as their forward press as this has the effect of getting the hands ahead of the ball at address.

I think the Nicklaus method of firming up the grip as an initial movement to start the swing is probably the best as it serves two purposes. First, it helps the player start the swing slowly and second, it prevents the player from gripping the club too tightly as he stands to the ball.

Jack Nicklaus at the finish of his swing. Notice the club hanging down over his left shoulder, an indication that the club has been kept on line throughout the swing.
Laura Baugh shows the importance of a smooth takeaway to set the rhythm of the swing.

Remember, the grip should be firm but not tight. If the grip is too tight at address it can only loosen during the swing.

Whatever forward press movement you use to trigger off your swing, always make sure it is one which helps you start the swing slowly. Your set-up to the ball can be perfect but if you start the swing in a jerky manner then the whole structure will collapse. Setting the tempo for your swing requires practice, but all good golfers agree that the slower the start to the swing, the better. Of course, temperaments differ and if you are a quick-moving person then your backswing may seem slow to you but appear very fast to a person who is slower and more deliberate in his actions.

The important thing is to build up momentum with the backswing and the only way to do that is to take the club back more slowly than you bring it down.

27

Chapter Four
Through the Green

The purpose of practising the fundamentals is to prepare yourself for actual play on the course. A great many players who have just taken up the game want to rush out onto the course with the aim of emulating the heroes they have seen on television. The results, however, are often sobering and disastrous and the player's confidence is shattered.

You must use your practice to build your confidence so that when you come to play you are fully aware of your abilities. Playing within those abilities and not being over-ambitious is the art of scoring well at golf. Bearing this in mind, you are now ready to step out onto the first tee and play.

This chapter is entitled 'Through the Green' because this is the term used in referring to all shots played up to the green, in other words the longer shots.

Your first shot is the drive or tee shot and it is the shot where you are allowed to place the ball on a tee-peg. The object of the drive is to hit the ball as far and as straight as you can down the fairway. The opening drive from the first tee brings great psychological pressures to bear on the golfer. First, because it is the first shot of the day and the player wants the shot to be a good one and second, more often than not, the player will be under the scrutiny of other golfers awaiting their turn to play. This situation can often induce panic in the player and in his haste to get the ordeal over he rushes his swing and the shot fails.

The best way to overcome this barrier is to work out a routine which should also be adopted for all shots. If you watch the top professionals you will see that they all have some kind of routine which they go through before each shot. Most of them will stand behind the ball and look down the fairway to give themselves a clear picture of where they want the ball to go. This 'visualizing

the shot' helps them and it can help you. Try and 'see' the shot in your mind before you hit it.

When a professional is ready to hit the ball, the first thing he will do is place the club pointing down the intended line of flight. Then and only then will he bring his feet and the rest of his body into position. Many amateur golfers approach the ball, get their feet and shoulders into position and then place the clubhead behind the ball with the result that they could, without realizing it, be aiming 20 yards to the left or right of their intended line.

You will also see professionals take a practice swing as part of their routine. This helps set the tempo for the shot and gives them a feel for the shot they want to hit.

If you adopt these factors into your

Right Tee up on the side nearest the trouble and plan each shot to make the next easier.

Below Extensive practice has given Tom Watson the confidence to repeat his swing under pressure. You can equal this position at the top, but you can't beat it.

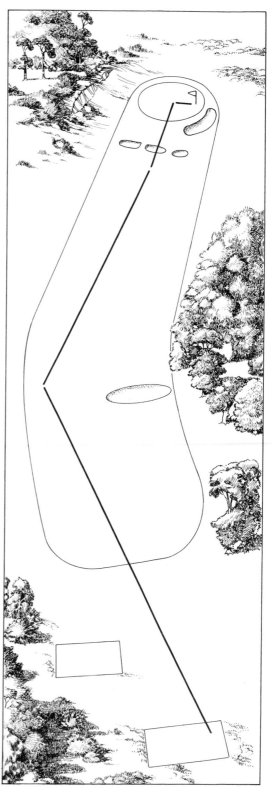

routine your first-tee nerves will not trouble you as much and if you continue your routine throughout the round, your confidence will gradually increase.

Bad shots are often caused by rushing

Opposite When your ball is in thick rough do not try the impossible, simply take a lofted iron and hit the ball back onto the fairway.

Two swings that epitomize the difference between aggression and safety. Arnold Palmer (above) has always believed the ball is there to be hit hard while Billy Casper (below) plays more conservatively. Both have been successful, but Palmer's golf is certainly more appealing to the spectator.

the shot and speeding up the swing so measure your movements and keep your swing slow and easy. It is one of the paradoxes of golf that the slower the start of the swing, the further the ball will travel when it is hit; the faster the start of the swing, the less the ball will travel.

Working backwards

The reason top professionals play many practice rounds on a course where a tournament is to be held is to get to know the course as well as possible. They want to know all the idiosyncrasies of the course before serious play gets under way. One of the tricks of their trade is one you

can adopt as well. I call it 'working backwards', but it can be referred to as 'course management' or even 'local knowledge'. When a top player is practising around a course, he will note yardages from landmarks on the edge of the fairway and he will note bunkers on each hole, particularly around the greens. He will note if there is trouble at the back of the greens and he will note which way each green slopes, whether from back to front or side to side. He will also note where the flagsticks or 'pins' are likely to be located during the tournament and from there he will work backwards to the tee. In other words, the pin positions will determine the most favourable angle to approach the green from the fairway and similarly, that will determine the best position for the drive to finish.

Although, to begin with, you may not be as accurate in your placement of shots, you can still use this method for planning your strategy on each hole. From the tee you should, in most cases, be able to see the pin. If it is on the right side of the green then the best angle of approach will be from the left side of the fairway. If you are unable to reach the green in two shots, then you should plan your second shot to finish on the side of the fairway that gives you the easiest approach to the pin

with your next shot. Always plan each shot so that the following shot is comparatively easier.

Playing a hole

Let us take a hypothetical hole some 380 yards long, it could even be the first hole on the course. On the right-hand side of the hole lies some thick woodland, but the left-hand side is fairly open. There is a bunker located on the right-hand side of the fairway about 200 yards from the tee. The hole progresses straightforwardly up to the green, but some 30 yards short of the green there is a row of cross-bunkers. The pin is located on the right side of the green and there is a bunker by the green on the same side.

Your strategy starts with the actual position you tee the ball. Always tee the ball up on the side nearest the trouble so that you are playing away from the danger. In this case you would tee the ball on the right-hand side of the tee and play away to the left half of the fairway where there is no trouble. Let us assume that you go through your routine successfully and your ball finishes in the light rough on the left side of the hole. You have 200 yards still to go to the green, but your ball is lying down in the grass. This is where you have to play intelligently. Remember, you had the advantage of hitting your drive off a tee-peg and your effort travelled 180 yards. For your second shot you have no such advantage and, furthermore, the ball is lying down in the grass. Even if you hit a four wood 100 per cent, it is unlikely you will carry those cross-bunkers and you are more likely to finish in them, making your next shot extremely difficult. The sensible thing to do is take a 5-iron and hit the ball short of the bunkers leaving yourself a simple pitch over the bunkers and onto the green with the chance of a single putt for your par four.

Play the percentages

Even top professionals realize that absolutely perfectly struck shots are few and far between. In fact, tournaments are usually won by the player who hits the fewest bad shots.

You are not a machine capable of hitting perfect shots every time. Learn to live with your mistakes, put them out of your mind and concentrate on the next shot. If you hit the ball into the rough, make sure you get the ball out onto the fairway with the next stroke. You have 14 clubs in your bag so use them sensibly. If your ball is in thick rough, don't haul out a wood and lunge at the ball in an attempt to hit the ball onto the green. The long grass will wrap itself around the club and ball will stay in the rough. Use a lofted iron instead since the narrower leading edge will cut through the grass and the ball will fly out.

Accuracy vs Power

Control of the long game is a vital ingredient in golf so control and accuracy should never be sacrificed in the quest for extra power. If you can hit the ball 200 yards up the fairway every time you will always have the measure of the player who hits every 10th drive miles up the middle of the fairway while the other nine are despatched on a journey into the woods from which they will never return.

The same applies to fairway woods and the long and medium irons. Controlled power is the ultimate aim and if you can achieve that then you are well on the way to becoming a good golfer. The best players, however, always play within themselves and rarely, if ever, hit a shot absolutely flat out. They would rather hit a gentle 5-iron to a green than flog a 6-iron, because they know that hitting flat out can disrupt their tempo and affect the shot.

As I have said, the object of the game is to get the ball in the hole in the least number of strokes and it is much easier to achieve that end from the middle of the fairway than from the middle of a gorse bush.

Chapter Five
Around the Green

In the previous chapter we talked about the longer shots for which the woods and long to medium irons, numbers three to six, would be used. In this chapter we shall discuss the short irons to be used from a distance of 140 yards from the green. These clubs (numbers seven to wedge and sand-wedge) are designed for accuracy with the object of hitting the ball as close to the pin as possible.

The short irons can be used for a variety of shots and although the swing basics remain the same, as you get nearer the green your backswing will shorten.

If you are 140 yards from the pin then you would probably hit a full 7-iron, from 130 yards a full 8-iron, from 120 yards a full 9-iron and from 100 yards a full wedge shot. If you are less than 100 yards from the pin, then you have to judge the length of your backswing to hit the ball the required distance. This judgment or 'feel' can only be acquired by practising with all the short irons.

Many golfers simply practise hitting the long shots with the woods or long irons and neglect to practise with the short irons. This is false economy as a chip shot

of 20 yards still counts as one stroke and therefore has the same value as a 250-yard drive. In fact the short game, as it is called, is more important than the long game for the simple reason that, during a round of golf, these clubs are used with far greater frequency than the longer clubs. In a perfect round of golf the player would put his ball on the green every time with the longer clubs, but such perfection is rare even among professionals. If you miss the green with your approach shot from the fairway and can get the ball in the hole with a chip and a putt, your scorecard will still show a par on the hole.

If your short game is of a high standard it relieves the pressures on your long game. A good short game can redeem your long game errors, but a poor short game can never be redeemed by the long game.

Getting it up and down

On the professional tournament circuit, getting the ball in the hole with a chip and a putt from anywhere off the green is called 'getting it up and down'. Professionals know the importance of being able to do this consistently as should you.

Outside of the full shots with the short irons in which the same swing is used as with the longer clubs, there are basically two types of short game shots you must have in your repertoire. These are the pitch shot and the chip shot. The pitch shot is used when the ball has to fly over an obstacle between you and the pin. The chip is used when there is no such obstacle.

In chapter two you will remember I mentioned that the position of the ball should always be on a line with the inside of the left heel and as the clubs become shorter then so the right foot moves nearer the left. This is the stance you should adopt for pitch shots and chips

The short irons, (right to left) numbers seven, eight, nine, wedge and sand-wedge, are used near the green.

with one slight variation. Your stance should be solid with your knees comfortably flexed, but your left foot should be turned to the left so your stance is slightly open. Both these shots are played with more emphasis on the hands and arms than the legs and the open stance helps reduce unwanted leg and body action.

The object of a pitch shot is to hit the ball high in the air so that it lands by the pin with very little roll. You may have seen professionals hit this type of shot and been amazed how the ball spins backwards when it lands. This backspin is imparted by hitting through the ball and squeezing the ball between the turf and the clubface so that the ball is spinning in a clockwise motion as it leaves the clubface. The grooves on the clubface assist in imparting this spin. The ball itself is covered in small dimples which balance it aerodynamically so that it cuts a path through the air. A totally smooth ball would fly poorly.

Backspin is the result of a well-hit shot and will occur in varying degrees. Do not try and deliberately impart backspin by smashing down on the ball in the belief that the harder you hit the ball the more backspin you will create. Backspin is obtained by good striking of the ball so initially you should concentrate on swinging the club onto and through the ball using the same measured tempo.

Let us assume you have a pitch of some 50 yards over a bunker which is 30 yards in front of you. For this shot you would use a 9-iron or a wedge. The loft on these clubs is quite sufficient to lift the ball in the air without any attempt by you to 'scoop' the ball. Scooping is the bane of the average golfer's short game as he feels he has to lift the ball into the air. This causes all kinds of horrors such as hitting the ground behind the ball or hitting the top of the ball and sending it skidding

The stance for chip and pitch shots: the left foot is drawn slightly back with the ball still opposite the inside of the left heel.

along the ground into the very bunker you are trying to clear.

A pitch shot is simply a full shot in miniature and all the same principles apply. Remember the basics and take the club back to around hip height, accelerate it through the ball and you will find the

Al Geiberger hits a pitch shot. Note the absence of body movement and how the hands and arms simply swing the club down through the ball.

No trace of 'scooping' from these three professionals. Roberto de Vicenzo, Peter Oosterhuis and Arnold Palmer all demonstrate how to let the clubhead throw up the ball.

shot flies into the air very satisfactorily. If you have a pitch shot of 75 yards you simply take the club back a little further and if you have a pitch shot of 20 yards you don't take the club back so far. You have to practise hard in order to discover how far you need to take the club back in order to hit the ball the distance required. Obtaining this feel for distance is the secret of a good short game and can only come by hitting many shots of this nature.

Let us now assume that you are faced with a shot of 20 yards to the pin with no obstacle in between. For this shot you put away your 9-iron or wedge and take a 7 or even a 6-iron. The object here is to keep the ball low to the ground and roll it up to the pin. You have much more control over a ball as it runs along the ground than you do when it is high in the air, therefore, for this shot when there is no need to hit the ball in the air, you use a club with less loft. Again, you have to practise in order to know how far to take the club back to hit the ball the distance required. But the

swing remains the same, a slow measured tempo with the club accelerating through the ball. Because the shot is shorter and the club less lofted, the trajectory of the ball will be lower and there will be less backspin on the ball. This means you must allow for the ball to roll considerably on landing. You should always try and land the ball on the cut portion of the green with a chip shot so that it bounces evenly and runs true. A good tip on chip shots is to pick a spot on the green where you want the ball to land, aim to land the ball on it and let it run up to the hole. Chips are played with the same slightly open stance and the shot is played entirely with the hands and arms with no body movement at all.

The chip shot from just off the green should be used when there is no obstacle between the player and the pin. This sequence shows the comparatively short backswing needed to hit the ball the correct distance, and note the absence of body movement.

Chapter Six
Putting

Putting is often called 'the game within a game' and many players feel that too much importance is attached to it, but I think that's just an excuse for poor putting!

Putting is a vital part of the game and when you consider that the putter is used more times during a round than any other club in the bag, then you can appreciate its importance.

There are basically two types of putter available, the centre-shafted putter and the blade putter. Blade putters are designed along the lines of a standard golf club with the shaft entering the clubhead at the hosel. Centre-shafted putters, as the name implies, have the shaft entering the club-head in the middle of the top of the head. Putters are manufactured in all shapes and sizes and as long as they conform with the regulations of the Royal and Ancient Golf Club or United States Golf Association then they are all perfectly legal.

Finding a putter which suits you is largely a matter of personal preference and what feels right to you in terms of balance, weight and length of shaft. Your build will dictate to a certain extent the type of putter you choose. If you are short and stocky you will probably favour a blade putter as these tend to be less upright in lie. Conversely, if you are tall then a centre-shafted putter with its upright lie may suit you.

Whatever putter you choose, stick with it and build your confidence with it. Don't chop and change in the belief that a new putter will work the magic—it's usually a case of bad workmen blaming their tools.

Putting technique
If you watch the professionals at a tournament you will see many different putting styles. Although the players may all look different as they stand to the ball, they are all concentrating on one thing. That is to return the face of the putter squarely to the ball along the intended line.

Most professionals change their grip slightly for putting and use the reverse overlap grip. For this grip, the index finger of the left-hand is laid over the fingers of the right-hand. This ensures that all the fingers of the right hand are on the shaft thereby giving a greater feel for the stroke. As with a full shot, the hands should work together as a unit and this reverse overlap grip will help you achieve that. Similarly, your feet should be square to the intended line with your

Four different types of putter: (from the right) centre-shaft, mallet, blade and offset centre-shaft.

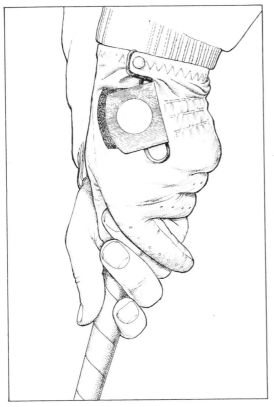

weight evenly balanced and the ball
positioned opposite the inner left heel.

Because the putting stroke is a relatively
small movement compared with a full
swing it is easy to forget that the foundations remain the same with particular
emphasis on the head. One of the keys to
good putting is to make sure your head is
over the ball and that it does not move
during the stroke.

For consistent putting you should
imagine that your putter is a pendulum
swinging in perfect time with your arms
and shoulders. The wrists play no role in
the stroke and should remain firm throughout. The stroke starts with the shoulders
and is transmitted through the arms to the
putter. This method gives your stroke an
even, smooth tempo and avoids any jerky
jabbing at the ball. Tempo is all-important
on the putting green and it takes practice
to establish it.

You will also need to practise in order

Top left The reverse overlap grip with the left index finger over the right-hand fingers.

Left Gary Player uses the reverse overlap grip with both thumbs pointing down the shaft — important for consistent putting.

Five top golfers with distinct putting styles. Green (left) crouches low over the ball. The great touch style of Ballesteros (above). The solid styles of Jacklin (centre), Morgan (above right) and Watson (right).

to find out how far you have to take the putter back in order to hit the ball the required distance. One good tip to help you with this is always to follow-through the same distance as you have taken the club back—if you take the putter back six inches then you follow-through six inches.

On the green

It is very rare in golf to come across a completely flat green so practically every putt you face will be on a green that slopes

As you approach a green look at the way the ground slopes in front and to the side of it. This sheltered green will take longer to dry out than greens set on exposed spots.

either uphill, downhill or sidehill–some putts may even travel on a combination of all three.

There is, however, no need to fear the slopes or 'borrows', as they are called, if you work on the simple principle that all putts are straight and it is only the borrows that cause them to curve. If you establish that in your mind then all you have to do is pick out the line the ball will follow along the ground and judge the speed at which the ball should travel.

Good putting starts with good thinking and planning. Remember our working backwards plan in chapter four and try and plan your approach shot to the green so that you are left with an uphill putt. Uphill putts are much more easy to judge than downhill putts. Of course, no golfer

can always leave himself an uphill putt but it helps to have that objective when you come to play your approach shot. As you walk up the fairway to your ball on the green, take note of which way the green slopes. You can often get a better perspective from a distance than from when you are actually standing on the green. Take note also of any overhanging trees around the greens as this indicates that the green will take longer to dry out from any overnight rain or dew and will therefore be slower in pace. The same applies to greens set in hollows. Greens that are raised and exposed will dry out more quickly and are likely to be of a faster pace.

When you are on the green, check whether you are putting with the grain of the grass or against the grain and also whether the grass is long or short, as these factors will determine the pace of the putt. Most courses have their greens mown regularly during the summer and always the day before or on the morning of a com-

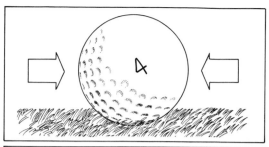

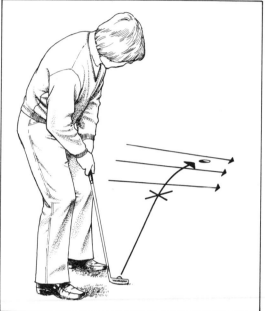

petition, so the greens will be fast in pace. When you have established the pace of your putt then you must decide on the line you want the ball to travel. Usually this is done by sighting behind the ball and the hole and seeing how the green slopes. Once you have decided the line, get on with hitting the putt–don't prevaricate because if you approach the putt in an indecisive manner you will almost certainly miss it. Remember the principle of every putt being straight and hit the ball along your chosen line. Don't fall into the trap of trying to help the ball along its

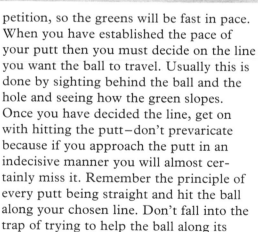

Top Check to see which way the grain of the grass runs. If it is with you the putt will be faster than if it is against you.

Centre On curving putts, speed is vital as the ball will become more susceptible to the borrow as it slows. Pick a spot and aim above the hole so that it at least has a chance of falling in and keep your head still!

Bottom On long putts, imagine you are putting into a 3 ft circle around the cup.

The 'Texas wedge' shot using a putter from the fringe of the green.

line by turning the putter face in an effort to compensate for the borrow. This particularly applies to sidehill putts with either a left to right borrow or a right to left borrow.

Sidehill putts are harder to judge because the speed at which the ball approaches the hole determines how much of the borrow the ball will take. If the ball is moving quickly as it approaches the hole, it will be less affected by the borrow than if it were travelling slowly. On a sidehill putt, the ball will never go in the hole if it is started off on a path that will take it below the hole; always try and make the ball travel towards the hole on the high side so that you at least have a chance of the ball taking the borrow and falling in. A good tip to remember on sidehill putts, and indeed all putts, is to pick a spot about six inches in front of the ball on your intended line and make sure the ball travels over that spot. Above all, resist the temptation to look up and watch the ball

fall into the hole because your eagerness will cause your head to move as you strike the ball and the putt will fail.

The longer the putt, the more important becomes the speed at which the ball is hit. It is no good hitting the putt on a good line only to see it shave the hole and go racing 10 feet past. On those long putts, think of putting into a three feet diameter bucket encircling the hole. You'll be surprised how many of your long putts finish close and some may actually go in. Sometimes you may find your ball has finished on the fringe of the green, maybe five feet from the edge of the actual putting surface. If the grass between your ball and the green is cut short and is growing towards the green, then you should use your putter for the shot. A putt should always be more accurate than a chip and there is no unwritten rule in golf to say you cannot use a putter from off the green. Some players use their putter from much further out, but the shot becomes risky as the ball is subject to being pulled up by longer grass or hitting a bump and being diverted. This shot is known as the

'Texas Wedge' and is particularly effective when the ground is hard.

Sam Snead's unique 'sidewinder' putting style has helped to cure his yips.

Now we come to the short putts. These are the putts you know you should hole but sometimes miss and the next becomes increasingly harder each time you miss one. Some very famous players have become so paralyzed over these putts that they are incapable of moving the putter away from the ball in anything less than a frenzied stab. This affliction is called the 'yips' and is quite common among golfers, particularly those who have played the game for many years. The yips are a psychological problem and are contracted through fear of missing a putt. The famous American professional San Snead was a chronic sufferer until he devised his unique side-saddle style in which he stands parallel to the line of the putt, facing the hole and using his putter with the right hand well down the shaft. Snead used to putt croquet style with his feet straddling the line but this style was made illegal so now he simply stands to one side of the line.

Snead's putting style certainly works

for him but if you use the pendulum style of putting with the shoulders acting as the fulcrum of your stroke then you are far less likely to suffer from the yips, which usually strike very wristy putters. In my golfing life, I have missed some short putts but I've also holed a great many long ones so things tend to balance out. It is as well to adopt a philosophical attitude to missed short putts and accept them as a quirk of fate and get on with the next shot.

If you approach each putt with a positive attitude then you are far more likely to hole it. Some players believe that they are going to hole every putt and with that kind of attitude they invariably hole a great many putts.

If you want to be a good putter then practise your stroke, weigh up the factors surrounding each putt, pick your line and be positive. Par allows you two putts on each green for a total of 36 in a round. If you can knock that down to 33 or 32, your handicap will soon come tumbling down.

Chapter Seven
Bunkers, Bushes and Other Encounters

By far the most common hazards on any golf course are bunkers or sand traps and it is inevitable that you will be required to hit your ball out of a bunker before your golfing career is very old. Many golfers view bunkers with much the same concern as a rabbit views a rattlesnake and consider it entirely appropriate that Hitler committed suicide in one!

There is no reason to fear these splashes of sand set around the course as man's ingenuity has devised a club specifically for the purpose of extracting golf balls from bunkers. It is called the sand-wedge and its deep face and thick sole are designed to plough through the sand and throw the ball up and out of the bunker. The rules of golf do not allow you to ground your club in a bunker or indeed any other hazard such as a ditch or stream.

Successful bunker play requires a slight change in technique from normal shots in as much as your stance will be slightly open to the intended line of flight. You still position the ball opposite the left heel but the left foot is drawn slightly back to give you that open stance. This stance helps reduce excessive body movement and will also cause you to take the club back outside the line and produce a slicing spin on the ball.

The bunker shot is the one shot in golf where you don't actually hit the ball. What you are trying to do is hit the sand behind the ball and continue on through the sand and under the ball with the force of the blow exploding the ball out in a shower of sand. This is why bunker shots are often called explosion shots. To achieve this effect, you must select a spot behind the ball where you think the club head should enter the sand and swing the club right

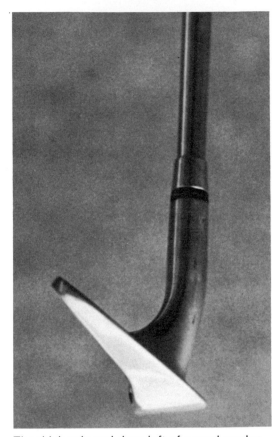

The thick sole and deep loft of a sand-wedge.

Opposite The address position for a normal bunker shot. The stance is slightly open with the left foot drawn back, the ball is played off the left heel and the club face is slightly open. When the ball is plugged in a bunker, the ball is played off the back foot and the club face is closed.

through the sand and on to a full finish.

Bunker shots require a great deal of practice in order to become really proficient. You will need to practise the length of backswing required in order to hit the ball a certain distance and you will also

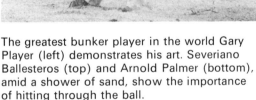

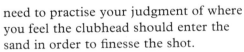

The greatest bunker player in the world Gary Player (left) demonstrates his art. Severiano Ballesteros (top) and Arnold Palmer (bottom), amid a shower of sand, show the importance of hitting through the ball.

need to practise your judgment of where you feel the clubhead should enter the sand in order to finesse the shot.

The keys to good bunker play are always to hit through the sand and don't quit on the shot. If you stop the clubhead on its path through and under the ball then you will throw up a lot of sand but no golf ball, but if you follow through then the ball will fly out. Explosion shots are used mainly for greenside bunkers where the object is to get the ball out of the bunker and close to the pin. The finest bunker player in the

world is Gary Player and he expects to get down in two from a greenside bunker every time—he even expects to hole a few bunker shots as well!

The other type of bunker shot is the long bunker shot when your ball has finished in a fairway bunker. For this shot you have to select an iron with enough loft to clear any overhanging lip the bunker may have. Never get too greedy for this shot and try and hit the ball with a club that hasn't enough loft in the mistaken belief that you will hit the ball 200 yards onto the green. The prime objective with a fairway bunker shot is to get the ball out of the bunker and into position for the next shot. For this shot you want to try and pick the ball cleanly off the top of the sand and to achieve this you must position the ball mid-way between your feet so the club hits the ball a descending blow. Remember you are still not allowed to ground your club so keep your swing smooth and at an even tempo as with all shots.

The bunker shots I have described are to be played when the ball is lying on the top of the sand and the sand itself is powdery. Sometimes, however, you will have to play the ball from wet sand and sometimes your ball will be plugged in the sand with only the top half of the ball showing. In wet sand you should take a normal stance as with a shot from grass and follow the procedure of picking a spot behind the ball and hitting right through. You will need to hit the ball harder from wet sand to cover the distance required. If your ball is plugged then you should close the face of your sand wedge slightly and hit hard behind the ball. From this shot, the ball will fly out with topspin so make allowances for the ball to run on once it lands.

You cannot practise bunker shots enough and the more you practise the more you will discover about how the ball reacts from bunkers. Knowing this will boost your confidence so that eventually you will regard bunker shots as just another challenge that you are capable of overcoming.

Woods, bushes and streams

Golf courses are usually beautiful examples of man's relationship with nature. The fairways glide between lines of trees and shrubs and occasionally there is the glint of water in the sunlight. But man, being a perverse creature, while appreciating nature's beauty frequently hits his golf ball into the trees and shrubs and water whereupon he roundly curses the very things he finds so aesthetically pleasing.

If your ball should fly into the bushes or water then the first thing to ascertain is whether the ball is lost. If it is then you

When the lip of a fairway bunker is as steep as this, the chief objective should be to get the ball out onto the fairway into position for the next shot.

simply play another ball under penalty according to the rules. If, however, the ball is found then you can either play it, take a drop under penalty or return to the original spot and play another ball, also under penalty. In this situation you must keep cool and weigh up the factors. The object here is to cut your losses. If you are in impenetrable jungle then it would be wise to return to the spot from where you hit the offending stroke and play another ball under penalty. If you are just in the edge of the trees and can swing a club at the ball unimpeded then it is worthwhile

47

Down in the forest something stirred! Greg Norman (left) and Peter Oosterhuis (right) extricate themselves from the jungle.

hitting the ball back to the fairway. To do this select a club such as a 4 or 5-iron and, gripping the club well down the shaft, knock the ball out. The lack of loft on the club will keep the ball low so that it flies under any overhanging branches. The system for bushes and trees should be that if you can swing the club unimpeded and can see a clear route back to the fairway then hit the ball, otherwise cut your losses and take relief under penalty.

Water on the golf course is another matter. You have virtually no chance of hitting your ball out of water unless it is on the very edge and you can see most of the ball above the water. Usually the ball is in so deep that you have to take a penalty anyway. Should your ball finish in deep rough then once again your objective is to get the ball back out to the fairway in one shot. Again, do not become over-ambitious and try to hit the ball miles. Thick rough wraps itself around the clubhead and twists it in your hands. Take a lofted club, such as a 9-iron, and position the ball in the middle of your stance. This will mean the club will strike the ball a descending blow and the loft of the club will pop the ball out. Always keep the swing smooth and don't try the impossible.

Wind and rain
Weather is always a factor in golf and wind, rain or a combination of both must be handled by the golfer. Playing in a strong wind tends to make most golfers

quicken their swing in an effort to combat
the gusts. This is fatal and can only
destroy the rhythm. Instead swing even
more slowly and let the wind help.

In a cross-wind you should allow for the
wind and aim slightly off-line to your
target and let the wind blow your ball back
on line. If you are hitting directly into the
wind then you want to try and keep the
ball low in which case you position the
ball towards the middle of your stance so
you hit it with a descending blow. If you
are playing with the wind directly behind
you then you want to get the ball high in
the air so that it flies further, particularly
with the tee shot. To achieve this, simply
position the ball slightly forward so that it
is opposite your left big toe. This will
mean you strike the ball as the club is
travelling upwards thereby giving the shot
a higher trajectory.

Right In this situation, don't try anything
fancy; just get the ball back to the fairway.
Below The essence of a water hazard is
shown on Augusta's 15th hole. This par five
hole presents the classic dilemma to the
professional after his tee shot. Should he go
for the green over the water or lay up short?

Playing in the rain is uncomfortable but sometimes cannot be avoided. You should be equipped with waterproofs and an umbrella as well as a towel and a spare left-hand glove. Keeping your hands and golf club grips dry is essential so that there is no slippage during the swing. Again, don't try and force the ball and keep the swing as slow and as smooth as you can. In these conditions you should grip the club down the shaft to give yourself more control over the shot. If you are playing a competition in the rain, don't get discouraged and remember that every other player is experiencing the same problems.

As your game becomes more advanced you will gradually learn which shots are effective in the wind and rain and will be able to adjust accordingly.

Above Yes, it used to rain in the good old days. Gene Sarazan drives from the seventh tee during the 1934 Open Championship at Royal St George's.

Below Uphill shots require the ball to be positioned more towards the left foot while on a downhill shot, the ball is placed more in the centre of the stance.

Uphill and downhill
You are going to encounter slopes and undulations wherever you play golf because courses would be very dull indeed if the ground was totally flat. Consequently, during a round your ball will invariably finish on a slope leaving you either an uphill shot, a downhill shot or a sidehill shot.

For an uphill shot, that is with the right foot below your left, the tendency is to fall back on the right foot as the swing is made. To avoid this, move your weight forward more onto the left foot and swing normally. The slope will also cause the ball to fly to the left when it is hit so to counteract this you must aim to the right of your target.

For a downhill shot, that is with your left foot lower than your right, the objective is to get the clubhead into the back of the ball as it is descending so you should position the ball more in the centre of your stance. Also you will need to flex your knees a little more to compensate for the slope. This slope will tend to make the ball fly to the right so again you must aim off-line, this time to the left of your target.

Now we come to sidehill lies of which there are two variations. The ball can either be below your feet or above your feet. If it is below your feet you will have to flex your knees more to reach the ball with the clubhead and you should position the ball more towards the centre of your stance. This shot will fly off to the right so allow for that. When the ball is above your feet you should also position the ball more towards the centre of your stance and you should allow for the ball to fly to the left.

For all sloping lies you should hold the club lower down the grip to give yourself greater control.

Heat and cold

Extreme heat or cold affects not only the way you play but also the performance of your golf ball. In hot weather the ball becomes more resilient and lively so that on landing it will run further as well as probably flying further through the air. In cold weather the ball is less resilient and therefore less responsive. If you are going out to play in cold weather it is a good idea to soak a couple of balls in some hot water to make them more resilient and

Golf in the idyllic setting of the Mount Irvine Bay Hotel course in Tobago where the temperature can soar into the 100s.

keep one in your pocket while you alternate them on different holes.

Golfers tend to tire towards the end of a round in hot weather so if you find this happening to you, slow down your swing and take a longer club for your shots to the green. When you are tired your muscles react less quickly so you have to pace your swing to allow for this.

In cold weather you will probably be playing in two or three sweaters and maybe a pair of waterproof trousers. These layers of clothing will restrict your swing considerably so be prepared for shorter shots, particularly drives. Try and keep your hands warm by wearing a pair of gloves between shots and try and keep moving. For winter golf, most golf clubs move the tees forward to compensate for the heavy conditions and they also play under 'winter rules' which allow you to clean and replace your ball on the fairway so causing less wear to the course. This is only a 'local rule' and does not apply in normal competition.

51

Chapter Eight

Putting it into Practice

Throughout this book, I have constantly exhorted you to practise the various aspects of the golf swing. As Gary Player once said: 'The more I practise, the luckier I get' and the same applies to you. Most golf clubs have a practice area, but it is no good simply going out there with a few balls and beating them aimlessly into the distance. Always practise with a purpose and always pick a target at which to aim, it may be only a distant tree or bush but use it to line up yourself in the correct manner. It also helps to lay a club down parallel to your intended line and then line your feet up against it and you can lay another club at right angles to the first one to assist you in positioning the ball correctly in your stance.

Whatever type of shot you wish to practise, always loosen up first with a short iron, perhaps a 7-iron, and gradually increase your swing arc until your muscles are fully stretched. Only then should you move down to the longer clubs because if you start with them your muscles won't be able to cope initially and your shots will be inconsistent.

If you are troubled by a particularly bad type of shot, a chronic slice or hook or topping the ball or any of the multitude of bad shots that can creep into your game, then it is worthwhile having a lesson from your professional. After your lesson put into practice what he has told you until the correct movements become ingrained in your swing. The worst thing to do is to practise your faults, so have a clear picture of what the professional has told you and

Severiano Ballesteros at practice, using his caddie in the distance as a marker. His flowing, attacking style of play is amply demonstrated in this sequence.

Positioning two clubs like this helps you line up correctly with the ball in the right position. Remember always to aim at a target while practising your shots.

Even top players like Nick Faldo consult a professional, in this case he is receiving attention from his mentor, Ian Connelly, who is helping him with his stance.

Some practice putting is vital before play.

remember that he has been trained to help you with your game.

If you are just starting golf you will find it difficult to judge how far to hit certain shots, especially the chips and pitches you need for an accurate short game. One of the best practice exercises to help you obtain this feel for a shot is to place a series of markers at varying distances away from you—a sweater or two or an umbrella will do. Place them at 20-yard intervals with the furthest one about 50 yards away from you. Then practise hitting some shots at the furthest marker,

some at the middle marker and some at the nearest marker. This will build up your feel for actual shots on the course. As you become more advanced you will be able to try hitting high shots, low shots and shots that spin from right to left and left to right. Use a 7-iron for this type of practice and once you have mastered these 'half-shots' you should be able to play them with practically every iron club.

Always leave yourself plenty of time for a practice session before you go out and play a round. If you arrive at the course with five minutes to spare before you are due to play it will take you about five holes to loosen up properly by which time your

Exultation from Tom Watson on the final green of the 1975 Open Championship at Carnoustie.

score will probably be in tatters. Loosen up with a dozen pitch shots, a dozen medium irons and a dozen drives. Then go to the practice putting green and get the feel of the pace of the greens. Just before you are due to tee off, swing your driver a few times to stretch your muscles again as they will have become cramped during your putting session.

Remember also the importance of practising your short game. Your club will almost certainly have a practice putting green so use it. Practise those little chips as well as putts of varying lengths. Finally, never practise in a high wind as you will start to make adjustments to combat the wind and your swing will suffer.

Practising attitudes

Of all the games, I believe golf places the most mental strain on the player. When you consider that in a three-hour round of golf, the player spends only two or three minutes actually striking the ball you can see the distractions that can occur in the remaining time. It is all too easy to let the mind wander and forget what you are supposed to be doing. That doesn't mean you should become a morose, solitary

figure on the course because golf is a social game and the pleasure of the company is an integral part of it. What it means is that you should use your time in between shots intelligently by assessing your next shot in your mind and preparing yourself for it. When you come to play the shot, your mind should be clear on what you are trying to do and your mental approach should be positive. If you attempt the shot with the mental attitude that you are bound to hit the ball into a bunker, out of bounds or into the rough then almost certainly you will, the negative seeds have been sown. If, on the other

Left You can almost feel the concentration Jack Nicklaus is applying to this putt. This ability to focus his attention exclusively on the shot in hand is his greatest asset.

Below The positive attitude of Gary Player makes him one of the game's fiercest competitors. This sequence shows Player's winning putt in the 1978 Masters. The emotion of the occasion is vividly captured as his partner, Severiano Ballesteros, comes across to congratulate him.

Right Remember, it's only a game!

hand, you tell yourself you are going to hit the ball onto the fairway or onto the green then your chances of doing so will be that much greater.

The power of positive thinking is a major factor in golf and should be brought to bear on every shot. If you happen to hit a bad shot don't dwell on it, put it out of your mind and focus your attention on the next shot and, above all, never give up. There are countless examples of players winning tournaments or matches when all seemed lost, so be positive and keep plugging away.

The end of the beginning

To paraphrase a famous British war-time leader, this book is not the end of your beginnings at golf, nor is it the beginning of the end. I hope your affair with golf will be as lasting and as enjoyable as mine for it is the game of a lifetime and like life itself, it will sometimes elate you, sometimes frustrate you but it will certainly never, never be dull.

Certainly you could ask no more from what is, after all, only a game.

Glossary

Ace The ultimate stroke in golf, a hole in one.
Albatross A hole completed in three strokes under par.
Arc The path the club completes through the swing.
Around the green The term used to describe shots played in the vicinity of the green.
Better-ball In which two partners play as a team, the best score of either counting. Also called four-ball.
Birdie A hole completed in one stroke under par.
Blind (hole or shot) A blind hole is one where the green cannot be seen from the tee. A blind shot is made when a high object prevents the player from seeing where he intends to hit the ball.
Bogey A hole completed in one stroke over par. A double-bogey is a hole completed in two strokes over par and so on.
Bunker A hazard filled with sand.
Bye The number of holes left to be played when a match is finished.
Caddie A person who carries the player's clubs.
Casual water A temporary pool of water on the golf course. When the course is waterlogged after heavy rain, the player is permitted to lift and drop his ball clear without penalty if the ball lies in casual water.
Chip A short shot to the green.
Concede A hole is conceded when one player has played so many shots it is impossible for him to win or halve it with his opponent. A player may also concede his opponent's putt if he feels the opponent is certain not to miss. Concessions take place only in match-play.
Dead When the ball lands so near the hole it is all but impossible for the player to miss the putt.
Divot The piece of turf removed when the ball is struck. All divots should be replaced to avoid damage to the course.
Dormie In match-play a player is dormie if he is as many holes ahead as there are left to play, e.g. if one player were three holes ahead with three to play he would be dormie three.
Draw The spin imparted to the ball so that it moves gradually from right to left.
Eagle A hole completed in two strokes under par.

Fade The spin imparted to the ball so that it moves gradually from left to right.
Fairway The cut portion of the course between the teeing ground and the green.
Flagstick The pole, usually with a small flag attached, placed in the hole to provide the

Above A blind hole with a marker post showing the line.

Right A drawn shot and a faded shot.

Below A ball lying dead to the hole.

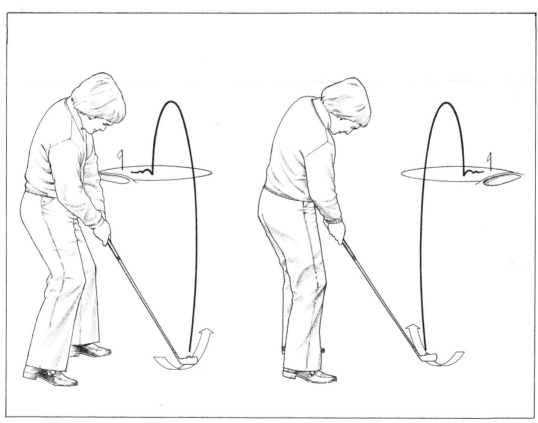

player with a target. Also called the pin.

Fore A shout of warning to anyone on the golf course indicating the ball is travelling in his direction.

Four-ball *see* better ball

Foursome A form of golf with two partners per team but instead of playing their own ball as in better ball, the partners play alternate shots with the same ball and drive at alternate holes.

Free drop Under certain conditions a player is allowed to drop the ball away without penalty. Check the rules of golf if in doubt.

Grip The position of the hands on the club and also the top part of the club where the hands are placed, which is usually covered in rubber or leather.

Green Each putting surface on the course.

Greensome A form of foursome in which two players play as a team but each player drives and then the team decides which ball to play in alternate strokes for the remainder of the hole.

Ground under repair Ground which has been repaired by the greenkeeper. The area is usually marked by a small notice.

Halved A hole is halved, or a match is halved, when the opponents are level, either in relation to strokes taken at each hole or at the end of a round.

Handicap The figure allotted to every player denoting the average difference between his score and the par of the course.

Hanging lie A downhill lie.

Hazard A bunker, ditch, stream or pond.

Hole The target on the green into which the ball must ultimately fall. The hole is $4\frac{1}{4}$ inches in diameter. Also the full distance between tee and green.

Holing-out Striking the ball into the hole.

Honour The preference given to the player whose turn it is to drive first. The honour on the first tee can be agreed but thereafter it goes to the player who had the lowest score at the previous hole. If a hole is halved, the player with the honour retains it.

Hook A shot which moves sharply in flight from right to left.

Hosel The point at which the shaft of the club enters the clubhead.

Ladies' tee The teeing ground used by women golfers, usually placed some distance forward from the men's tee.

Lateral water hazard A ditch or stream

which, when viewed from the fairway, runs parallel to a hole instead of across it.

Lift and drop under penalty If a ball has to be lifted because it is impossible to play it from where it lies, the player is permitted to lift and drop under the penalty laid down by the rules. The procedure for dropping should be that the player faces the hole and drops the ball over his shoulder.

Local rules The rules of golf apply everywhere golf is played but all clubs have additional rules on certain points pertaining to the locality of the club.

Loft The angle at which the clubhead lies in relation to the shaft.

Lost ball Players are allowed to look for five minutes for a lost ball but after that time has elapsed they have to deem the ball lost and play another according to the rules.

Match-play When opponents play in pairs the winner is the player who finishes more holes ahead than there are left to play.

Medal-play When the player counts the number of strokes taken during the round. Also called stroke-play.

Obstructions Objects, either movable or immovable, which prevent the playing of a shot.

Out of bounds When the ball is hit over the boundaries of the course or hole, thus incurring a penalty.

Outside agency Any person or animal not

involved in the game who obstructs or moves the ball.

Par The score allocated to a hole or to a course, based on the terrain, the length and the difficulty. Also called standard scratch score.

Partner The person with whom one plays either as individuals or as a team.

Penalty When a shot finishes in a lie from which the ball is unplayable, out of bounds or lost, then a penalty is incurred according to the rules. Penalties can also be incurred for infringement of the rules.

Pitch A high, lofted shot played from near the green.

Playing out of turn In match-play, if a golfer plays before it is his turn to play either from the tee or fairway, his opponent may request that the ball be called back and the shot played again.

Playing preferred lies *see* winter rules

Pull A shot that flies directly to the left with no hook spin; to hit a shot directly to the left with no hook spin.

Push A shot that flies directly to the right with no slice spin; to hit a shot directly to the right with no slice spin.

Putt The stroke used on the greens and played with a putter.

Round Completing all the holes on the course, usually 18 holes.

Rub of the green Interference with the ball that is put down to fate.

Scorecard The card taken out and filled in by golfers in stroke-play. It has to be filled in by the player's partner, checked and signed by both players.

Slice A shot which moves sharply in flight from left to right.

Standard scratch score *see* par

Stroke The striking of the ball.

Stroke-play *see* medal-play

Tee The wooden or plastic peg on which the ball is placed prior to driving off. Also the teeing ground.

Tee-markers Metal or plastic objects used to mark the forward limits of the teeing ground.

Through the green The term used in referring to the whole area of the course except the teeing ground, the putting green and all hazards on the course. The term is also used when a player hits a shot too boldly so that it runs over the back of the green.

Trap Also called a bunker.

Winter rules Special rules for play during the months when the course is wet or frost-bound. Winter rules allow the ball to be lifted, cleaned and placed in a better lie without penalty, thereby lessening damage to the course. Also called playing preferred lies.

Left The procedure for dropping the ball.

Below The teeing ground.

Index

Numbers in *italics* refer to illustrations. The glossary has not been indexed.